The Ummah

Between Wilāyat al-Faqīh
and Marjiʿiyyat al-Taqlīd

In the Thought of
Āyatullāh Sayyid Khumaynī

Copyright

ISBN: 978-1-956276-50-3
Printed and published by al-Burāq Publications.
Translated and annotated by al-Burāq Publications. Where needed, context and transliterations were added. Some minor edits were made to the translated Arabic text.

Ordering Information
We offer discounts and promotions for wholesale purchases, non-profit organizations, and other educational institutions. Contact us at the email below for further information.

www.al-Buraq.org
publications@al-Buraq.org

First Edition | June 2024

Dedication

The publication of this book was made possible through the generous support of our donors.

Please recite *Sūrat al-Fātihah* and ask God for the Divine reward (*thawāb*) to be conferred upon the donors and also the souls of all the deceased in whose memory their loved ones have contributed graciously towards the publication of *The Ummah: Between Wilāyat al-Faqīh and Marjiʿiyyat al-Taqlīd*.

We begin by giving all praise and thanks to God ﷻ for giving us the *tawfīq* to translate this book. He has guided us and without Him, we would not have been guided to the straight path embodied by the Prophet Muḥammad ﷺ and the Ahl al-Bayt عليهم السلام.

This book is dedicated to all the scholars, martyrs and believers who worked tirelessly to promote the pure Muḥammadan path.

We want to also give our thanks and appreciation to all believers from around the world and acknowledge the team which helped al-Burāq Publications complete this work, spending countless hours to make its publication possible. Please recite Sūrat al-Fātiḥah on behalf of them, their families, and their marḥūmīn.

Du‘ā’ al-Ḥujjah

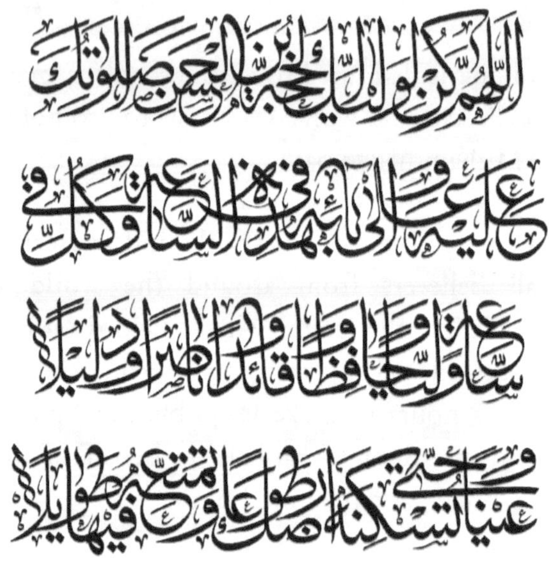

O God, be, for Your representative, the Ḥujjat (proof), son of al-Ḥasan, Your blessings be upon him and his forefathers, in this hour and in every hour: a guardian, a protector, a leader, a helper, a proof, and an eye - until You make him live on the Earth, in obedience (to You), and cause him to live in it for a long time.

Terms of Respect

The following Arabic phrases have been used throughout this book in their respective places to show the reverence which the noble personalities deserve.

Used for God, meaning:
Exalted and Sublime (Perfect) is He

Used for Prophet Muḥammad, meaning:
Blessings from God be upon him and his family

Used for a man (singular) of a high status, meaning:
Peace be upon him

Used for a woman (singular) of a high status, meaning:
Peace be upon her

Used for men/women (dual) of a high status, meaning:
Peace be upon them both

Used for men and/or women (plural) of a high status, meaning:
Peace be upon them all

Used for Imām Muḥammad al-Mahdī, meaning:
May God hasten his return

Used for a deceased scholar, meaning:
May his resting [burial] place remain pure

Transliteration Table

The method of transliteration of Islāmic terminology from the Arabic language has been carried out according to the standard transliteration table below.

ء	ʾ	ر	r	ف	f
ا	a	ز	z	ق	q
ب	b	س	s	ك	k
ت	t	ش	sh	ل	l
ث	th	ص	ṣ	م	m
ج	j	ض	ḍ	ن	n
ح	ḥ	ط	ṭ	و	w
خ	kh	ظ	ẓ	ه	h
د	d	ع	ʿ	ي	y
ذ	dh	غ	gh		

Long Vowels

ا	ā	و	ū	ي	ī

Short Vowels

◌َ	a	◌ُ	u	◌ِ	i

Table of Contents

Preface

In the Name of God, the Beneficent, the Merciful

The status of the Marji'iyyat is deeply embedded in the Shī'ī core, and it manifests in the widespread inquiry—amongst the followers of this creed—about the jurist eligible for emulation (*taqlīd*) and his religious rulings. It is also manifested in religious mothers and fathers' guidance of their daughters and sons towards the exigency of taqlīd starting at the age of religious duty.

Nonetheless, we do not observe this adherence or this relationship with the jurist as a guardian. On the contrary, some of the followers of this sect—some seminary scholars—were doubtful of the general Guardianship of the Jurist that was adopted by the Islāmic revolution in Irān led by Āyatullāh Sayyid Rūḥullāh Mūsawī Khumaynī ﷺ as the Guardian Jurist.

The interesting thing is that Āyatullāh Sayyid Khumaynī ﷺ declared, during his seminary lectures in Najaf in the sixties of the previous century, that the Guardianship of the Jurist is necessary and evident, and it does not need to be proved for anyone knowledgeable of the Islāmic ideology and provisions. For, religiously, it is as obvious as emulation (*taqlīd*). This raises several questions which we aim to answer in the following chapters, such as:

1. What does it mean to say that the Guardianship of the Jurist is a religious axiom for a religious scholar?

2. If the Guardianship of the Jurist is self-evident, as mentioned above, then where is this proposition in the words of Shīʿī jurists throughout the ages?

3. What is the scope and extent of the Guardianship of the Jurist according to Āyatullāh Sayyid Khumaynī's proposal?

4. If the Guardian of the Jurist concept is embedded in the Shīʿī jurists, as per its evident basis, what is its subsequent alienation?

5. What purpose did Āyatullāh Sayyid Khumaynī aim to achieve by emphasizing the evident basis of the Guardianship of the Jurist for an Islāmic scholar?

The Self-Evidence of the Jurist's Guardianship

In his book *Ḥukūmat Islāmiyyah* (*Islāmic Government*) which comprised lectures he had delivered in the seminary of Najaf after being exiled from Irān, Āyatullāh Sayyid Khumaynī said: "The guardianship of the jurist (Wilāyat al-Faqīh) is a clear rational concept that does not require evidence, in the sense that whoever knows the provisions and ideologies of Islām will recognize its evidence. However, the status quo of the Islāmic community and our academic institutions – in particular – keeps this subject far away from people's minds, to the extent that it now requires proof."[1]

This text includes two contradictory points:

1. The jurist's guardianship is self-evident; however, its evidence is not general for all people; it is rather evident for those knowledgeable in Islāmic provisions and theology. Therefore, it is a specific axiom.

---

[1] Khumaynī, Āyatullāh Sayyid Rūḥullāh Mūsawī, *Ḥukūmat Islāmiyyah*, 2nd edition, Beirut, Āyatullāh Sayyid Khumaynī's cultural center, 1390 AH, p. 9.

2. The guardianship of the jurist during the aforementioned text (the sixties of the past century) wasn't evident. It was rather distant from the scholars' minds, and proving it required evidence.

In his analysis, Āyatullāh Sayyid Khumaynī emphasizes that the reason for this change was not intellectual, as is the case with changes that occur with scientific theories. The reason was rather related to the status quo of the Islāmic community and the academic institutions and seminaries in particular.

Proof for the Self-Evident Nature of the Jurist's Guardianship

Some may object to this subtitle, considering that proof correlates with evidence and therefore counters the self-evidence. An evident thing does not need evidence to prove it. That is why scholars used the term 'alarm' instead of proof for that which indicates the axiom. Nonetheless, what makes speech easy is that Āyatullāh Sayyid Khumaynī, in his book *Islāmic Government*, did not raise the concept of the guardianship of the jurist as a general axiom but rather as a specific axiom for those who are knowledgeable in the

Islāmic provisions and ideologies. In other words, what Āyatullāh Sayyid Khumaynī raised as proof for the guardianship of the jurist was based on the intellect that is aware of Islāmic theology and observant of the Islāmic Sharīʿa – even though we will briefly refer to the Imām's proof as 'rational evidence.' Based on the elaboration above on being knowledgeable in Islāmic provisions and ideologies, we will clarify, below, the indicators raised by the Imām:

1. The Indication of Islāmic Provisions to the
    Guardianship of the Jurist

We can say that Āyatullāh Sayyid Khumaynī established proof for the guardianship of the jurist that carries within it several issues:

The first issue: Islām is a religion of government. In pursuit of proving this proposition, Āyatullāh Sayyid Khumaynī presents in his book *Islāmic Government* examples of Islāmic provisions that indicate the fact that Islām is a religion of government, which are:

a. The financial provisions that generate huge amounts of money only suit a governmental treasury. Some of the financial headlines pointed out by the Imām are Khums, Alms (Zakāt), and al-Kharāj..., and in regards to Khums, he said: "The Khums is a huge resource which brings to the treasury a large amount of money that constitutes the largest portion thereof. According to our tradition, the Khums are taken from all the gains, benefits, and profits in agriculture, commerce, industry, and other industries. The grocer (who sells vegetables) also contributes by paying the Khums if he makes money that exceeds his annual needs, which aligns with the religious provisions regarding spending and expenditure. Moreover, the salesman, manufacturer, car driver, ship captain, and pilot contribute to the Khums. All those people, amongst others, must pay one-fifth of the excess profit to the Imām ﷻ or his representative, who must add it to the treasury.

It is rather evident that this huge resource is used to run the affairs of the Islāmic community and fulfill its required needs.

Moreover, if we want to calculate the Khums of the overall profits in the Islāmic state or all across the world – if countries thereof abide by Islām – then we will realize that these huge amounts of money do not merely serve to fulfill the needs of a Sayyid (a person who belongs to the paternal lineage of the Prophet or Imāms) or a knowledge seeker. The issue is much greater and more expansive than this, for it serves to fulfill the needs of the entire nation. Moreover, when the Islāmic state materializes, it must carry out its affairs by resorting to the sums collected from Khums, Alms (Zakāt), penalties (al-Jizyah), and al-Kharāj.

When did Sayyids ever need such amounts of money? The Khums of Baghdād's market are sufficient to cover the needs of all Sayyids and the expenses of all religious seminaries and all the poor Muslims, notwithstanding the markets in Tehrān, Istānbūl, and al-Qāhirah (Cairo). For, a budget of such size is meant to serve a huge nation and the crucial needs of the people, in addition to carrying out the public health, cultural, educational, defensive, and architectural services."[2]

b. The defense provisions, considering that they are only appropriate for a government that shoulders the responsibility of defending Islām

---

[2] Ibid., p. 32-33.

and Muslims. Āyatullāh Sayyid Khumaynī said: "Islām ruled that it is mandatory to prepare, get equipped and be ready even in times of peace as per God's ۞ saying:

﴿وَأَعِدّوا لَهُم مَا اسْتَطَعْتُم مِن قُوَّةٍ وَمِن رِباطِ الخَيْلِ تُرهِبونَ بِهِ عَدُوَّ اللَّهِ وَعَدُوَّكُم﴾

﴾wa-'a'iddū lahum mā staṭa'tum min quwwatin wa-min ribāṭi l-khayli turhibūna bihī 'aduwwa llāhi wa-'aduwwakum﴿

﴾Prepare against them whatever you can of [military] power and war-horses, awing thereby the enemy of God, and your enemy﴿[3]

c. The provisions related to limits, blood money, and penalties, and this case resembles its precedent. The Imām said, "These provisions cannot be implemented except by governmental powers. Through these powers, blood money is taken from the perpetrator and paid to its right-owners, and through them, limits are enforced. Moreover, penalties are

---

[3] Sūrat al-Anfāl, Verse 60.

carried out under the supervision and monitoring of the religious ruler."[4]

From these examples, Āyatullāh Sayyid Khumaynī concluded the first issue in his proof for the guardianship of the jurist, which is that Islām is a religion of government. He then adds two other issues, which are:

The second issue is that a government needs a ruler who can govern in light of Islām. Therefore, he must know its laws, i.e., a jurist.[5], in addition to being qualified politically, economically, administratively, and otherwise, and trustworthy in implementing these provisions – thus just.

In a nutshell, a government needs a competent, just, and juristic ruler.

---

[4] Khumaynī, Āyatullāh Sayyid Rūḥullāh Mūsawī, *Ḥukūmat Islāmiyyah*, p. 35.

[5] In *Ḥukūmat Islāmiyyah*, Āyatullāh Sayyid Khumaynī raised a piece of evidence for the requirement of jurisprudence in the guardian; if he emulates another marjiʿ, then his government loses stature and will therefore be weak. We have discussed this proof in our book *Wilāyat al-Faqīh Bayn al-Badāhah wal-Ikhtilāf*, p. 96-97.

The third issue: When this competent and just jurist governs in light of his understanding of Islām and observance of the community's interests, the nation must obey him; otherwise, the two preceding foundations would be meaningless.

These three issues verify the guardianship of the competent and just jurist over the nation. Moreover, this result is evident and needless of any evidence, as mentioned in the text above and as the Imām mentioned in his book al-Bayʻ (The Sale): "... Therefore, and after imagining the parties of the case, the guardianship of the jurist is not a theoretical thing that requires proof."[6]

2. The Indication of Islāmic Theologies to the Guardianship of the Jurist

Muslims do not debate the guardianship of the Prophet ﷺ over the Muslim community, for he is the most perfect amongst them in knowledge, competence, and trustworthiness. Likewise, Imāmate Shīʻīs do not debate the guardianship of their Imāms over the Muslim community, as they are the most perfect after the Messenger of God ﷺ

---

[6] Khumaynī, Āyatullāh Sayyid Rūḥullāh Mūsawī, *Kitāb al-Bayʻ*, 4th edition, Qum, Ismāʻīliyyān, 1410 AH, p. 467.

regarding the three traits above. However, the debate arises in regards to the continuity of the guardianship after the Messenger of God ﷺ for non-Shīʿīs and after the occultation of Imām al-Mahdī ﷿ for Twelver Shīʿīs.

Therefore, Āyatullāh Sayyid Khumaynī did not stop presenting examples related to Islāmic provisions; he added a clear theological issue: the immortality of these provisions and, accordingly, the need for implementing them in all ages. Āyatullāh Sayyid Khumaynī continued this statement by referring to the well-known ḥadith: "What is permissible (ḥalāl) by Muḥammad remains permissible (ḥalāl) until the day of Resurrection, and what is forbidden (forbidden) by him remains forbidden until the day of Resurrection."[7] To emphasize the fact that the examples he presented were not specific to the time of the Messenger of God ﷺ or the Imāms of Ahl al-Bayt ﵇, they are rather as immortal as Islām. Āyatullāh Sayyid Khumaynī said:

---

[7] al-Ḥurr al-ʿĀmilī, Shaykh Muḥammad, *Wasāʾil al-Shīʿa*, verified by Sayyid Muḥammad Riḍā al-Jalālī, 2nd edition, Qum, Institute of Ahl al-Bayt, 1414 AH, Vol. 30, p. 196.

"It is evident that the necessity of executing the provisions was not specific to the age of the Prophet ﷺ; the necessity is continuous because Islām is not limited to a time or place, as it is immortal. Therefore, it must be implemented, executed, and abided by forever. Moreover, if what is permissible by Muḥammad remains permissible until the day of Resurrection and what is forbidden by him remains forbidden until the day of Resurrection, then his limits must not be suspended, his teachings must not be abandoned, punishment must not be forsaken, financial taxes must not be stopped and defending the Muslim nation and their lands must not be abandoned. The belief that Islām came for a specific period or to a specific place conflicts with the necessities of Islāmic theologies. Moreover, since implementing the provisions after the Messenger of God ﷺ – and forever – is of the necessities of life, a government with the traits of an executive and managerial power becomes necessary."[8]

---

[8] Khumaynī, Āyatullāh Sayyid Rūḥullāh Mūsawī, *Ḥukūmat Islāmiyyah*, p. 28-29.

The Proof of Preserving Public Order

Āyatullāh Sayyid Khumaynī was not satisfied with this theological addition to the indicators of the Islāmic provisions above; he presented a separate rational proof for the necessity of an Islāmic government from which the first introduction to the preceding complex indicator (to the jurist's guardianship) is established. This indicator can be referred to as the necessity of preserving public order, which can be explained as follows: God, the Wise, wanted his creation to reach their perfection. For this purpose, He sent down the Sharīʿa so that man could reach perfection in the light by abiding by it. Because perfection has two aspects, the individual and the social, the social aspect – in light of the social Islāmic provisions – requires the presence of someone to organize it. Otherwise, without this organizer, an imbalance will occur within the community. Thus, the blessed Messenger ﷺ was that organizer.

The Shīʿīs concluded the necessity of an Imām after the Messenger of God ﷺ from the fact that leaving the community without an organizer would lead to an imbalance in its public order.

Shīʿī scholars suggested that identifying the guardian by name is related to his role in preserving the Prophetic Sunnah and disseminating it, which rationally requires the presence of an infallible and, accordingly, divine guidance towards him. Regarding the position of social leadership, including all its diverse aspects, rationality does not demand infallibility thereof; it rather guides towards the necessity of having the leader be the perfect person amongst others regarding knowledge, competence, and trustworthiness. Even though both conditions in the age of the Imāms ﷯ would be met, since the infallible is simultaneously the most perfect and therefore the religious reference in regards to the Prophetic Sunnah will not be separate from the social leadership, nonetheless, the question is raised during the occultation of Imām al-Mahdī ﷯ – specifically 329 AH which is the starting year of the great occultation. Is it possible that God, the Wise, will hide Imām al-Mahdī ﷯ without having someone specified by name after the occultation of the Imām, who shall guide towards the ruling guardian during the period of the occultation, even if it is only through providing qualifications?

For the same reason, if we want to preserve a unified approach and harmony among Imāmate Shīʿīs, the answer must be yes.

If we say that guidance towards a guardian is unnecessary, then the speaker will follow the Imāmate Shīʿī approach until 329 AH. As for the period afterward, the question is raised regarding the extent of harmonization between this statement and the Imāmate Shīʿī approach, which must be unified.

According to the above, Āyatullāh Sayyid Khumaynī's statement on the evidence of the jurist's guardianship of the knowledgeable person in Islāmic provisions and theologies has been clarified. This now triggers the discussion of the other questions raised in the introduction, some of which were: If the jurist's guardianship was self-evident, as mentioned above, where is this proposition amongst the words of the Shīʿī jurists throughout the ages? This will be answered in the following chapter.

The Historical Nature of the Jurist's Guardianship

He, who studies the books of Shīʿī jurists, realizes that the proposition of the jurist's guardianship is widely mentioned in their books regardless of the diversity of its scopes. In this chapter, we will limit our presentation to two of these scopes which are the scopes of enacting limitations and public interest.

The Scope of Enacting Limitations

This scope is more advanced than the guardianship of the judicial system. The latter can be restricted to the jurist's ruling in front of the conflicting parties, which is binding for them, as mentioned in some credible narrations by Shīʿī scholars.[9] Executing limits such as the severing of the hand, stoning, and its likes require—in addition to a jurist's ruling—executive necessities such as the presence of a location where those sentenced to imprisonment can be imprisoned. This requires a security system such as security guards and a logistics system to attend to the prisoners' needs, and the same applies to the execution of other

---

[9] *Maqbūlat ʿUmar b. Ḥanẓala*: Kulaynī, Shaykh Muḥammad b. Yaʿqūb, *al-Kāfī*, 5th edition, Tehrān, Dār al-Kutub al-Islāmiyyah, 1363 AH, Vol. 1, p. 67, ḥadith 10.

rulings, which implies a sort of executive government regardless of its size.

Several Shīʿī jurists adopted the guardianship of the jurist over the enactment of limitations, amongst whom were:

1. Shaykh al-Mufīd (Shaykh Muḥammad b. Muḥammad b. al-Nuʿmān; 413 AH)

He said, "As for the enactment of limitations, it belongs to the sultan of Islām who is denoted by God ﷻ; and they are the Imāms of guidance from the progeny of Muḥammad ﷺ and whomever they have denoted for this purpose from amongst princes and rulers. Moreover, they delegated the investigation to jurists from amongst their followers where possible..."[10]

2. al-Ḥillī, ʿAllāmah al-Ḥasan b. Yūsuf (726 AH)

After presenting the accepted narration by ʿUmar b. Ḥanẓala on behalf of Imām al-Ṣādiq ﷺ, he said: "In addition to other narrations that imply the permissibility of ruling for jurists, and it is general -

----

[10] Mufīd, Shaykh Muḥammad, *al-Muqniʿah,*, 2nd edition, verified and published by the Institute of Islāmic Press, Qum, 1410 AH, p. 810.

thus applicable - for executing limits and other matters."[11]

He also said "... It has been proven that jurists are the ones who are entitled to rule amongst people; likewise, they are entitled to enact limitations. Moreover, because the suspension of limits during the occultation of the Imām - despite being capable of executing them – causes corruption, it becomes permissible. Moreover, in my opinion, it is quite a strong (proposition)."[12]

3. Shahīd al-Awwal: The First Martyr (876 AH)

He said that limitations and reinforcements belong to the Imām ﷺ and his representative, even in general situations. Therefore, during the occultation period, the denoted jurist can – in

---

[11] Ḥillī, ʿAllāmah Ḥasan b. Yūsuf, *Mukhtalaf al-Shīʿa fī Aḥkām al-Sharīʿa*, verified and published by the Institute of Islāmic Press, 1st edition, 413 AH, Vol. 4, p. 464.

[12] Ḥillī, ʿAllāmah Ḥasan b. Yūsuf, *Muntahā al-Ṭalab*, (L.T), (L.M), (L.T), Vol. 2, p. 995.

judicial matters – enact (these limitations) where it is possible."[13]

Before moving to the second scope, we emphasize the fact that what we mentioned regarding the guardianship of the jurist over enacting limitations does not conflict with adopting the idea that the guardianship of the jurist has a greater scope than that concerning those jurists, as indicated by the saying above by Allāma al-Ḥillī: "for enacting limitations and other matters." Likewise, we observe Shahīd al-Awwal's description of the jurist who is the representative of the Immaculate (Imām), where he described him as the governor of the Sharīʿa, which he mentioned by saying: "This is because the social gathering is one of the necessities of the dutiful, and it causes conflict. Therefore, there must be a firm settler, which is the Sharīʿa. Moreover, it must have a governor who is the Imām and his representatives."[14] The sayings above

---

13 Shahīd al-Awwal, Lectures, verified and published by the Institute of Islāmic Press, 1st edition, Qum, 1414 AH, Vol. 2, p. 47.

14 Shahīd al-Awwal, Muḥammad al-Shāmī al-ʿĀmilī al-Jizzīnī, *al-Qawāʿid wal-Fawāʾid*, (L.T.), Qum, publishings of al-Mufīd Library, Vol. 1, p. 38

were cited under the title of enacting limitations because they were certainly declared in their words.

The Scope of Public Interest

This scope is wide and inclusive of the execution of limits and other interests, referred to as general guardianship. Many jurists adopted this scope, some of whom we mention here:

1. Muḥaqqiq[15] Karakī (940 AH)

He said: "Our companions (May God be pleased with them) agreed that a just jurist who believes in the Imāmate and possesses the conditions that entitle him to establish a legal ruling – who is referred to as a Mujtahid.[16] In establishing legal rulings, the Imāms of guidance ﷺ assign a representative during the occultation period in all the matters included in the representation.[17]

---

[15] Investigator or researcher.

[16] A mujtahid is a jurist who uses independent reasoning to find a solution to a legal question.

[17] Al-Karakī, ʿAlī, the letters of al-Karakī, verified by Muḥammad al-Ḥassūn, 1st edition, Qum, Āyatullāh Marʿashī Najafī Library, 1409 AH, Vol. 1, p. 142.

2.   Shahīd al-Thānī: The Second Martyr (965 AH)

He said: "... the intended meaning behind the term jurist in the sense of guardianship is: he who possesses the conditions that entitle him to establish a legal ruling..., thus he is assigned for the sake of (managing) the general affairs."[18]

3.   Muḥaqqiq Narāqī (1245 AH)

He said: "All which the Prophet ﷺ and the Imām ؏ - who are the sultans of mankind and the forts of Islām – had guardianship over, and which belonged to them, is an entitlement of the jurist as well, except that which was excluded by evidence concluded from unanimity or text or otherwise."[19]

4.   Shaykh Muḥammad Ḥasan al-Najafī (1266 AH)

He said, "... nay if it were not for the generalization of guardianship, many affairs related to their

---

[18] Shahīd Thānī, Zayn al-Dīn al-ʿAmilī al-Jubaʿī, *Masālik al-Afhām ilā Tanqīḥ Sharāiʿ al-Islām*, verified and published.

[19] Muḥaqqiq Narāqī, Aḥmad, *ʿAwāʾid al-Ayyām*, verified by the center of Islāmic studies and research, 1st edition, (L.M.), the publishing center under the office of Islāmic press, 1417 AH, p. 536.

followers would be suspended. Therefore, it is strange that some people are perplexed by that. It is as if they had not understood anything from jurisprudence, nor had they comprehended anything from their words and symbols, nor had they reflected upon their purpose behind saying: "I have assigned him as a ruler over you," and a judge, a proof, a vicegerent and its likes which imply the will to organize the occultation period for their followers... All in all, the issue is evident and needless of proof."[20]

5. Āyatullāh Muḥammad Ḥusayn Nā'īnī (1315 AH)

He said, "...and by the principles of our creed, whereby we believe that the nation's affairs and its politics are delegated to the general representatives during the occultation period."[21]

---

[20] al-Najafī, Shaykh Muḥammad Ḥasan, *Jawāhir al-Kalām fī Sharḥ Sharāiʿ al-Islām*, verified by ʿAbbās al-Qawjānī, 3rd edition, Tehrān, Dār al-Kutub al-Islāmiyyah, 1362 AH, Vol. 21, p. 397.

[21] Al-Mīrzā al-Nā'īnī, Muḥammad Ḥusayn, *Tanbīh al-ʿUmma wa Tanzīh al-Millah*, translated by ʿAbd al-Ḥusayn al-Najaf, (L.T.), Qum, (L.N.), (L.T.), p. 107.

6. Shaykh Muḥammad Riḍā al-Muẓaffar (1383 AH)

He said: "Our theological belief in the Mujtahid who possesses the required conditions is that he is the representative of the Imām ﷺ during the occultation period and the absolute ruler and Chief... nay he has the general guardianship which makes him the reference in matters of government, decision making and judicial ruling... Moreover, anyone is prohibited from executing limits and reinforcements save upon his command and ruling."[22]

This is a sample of the words expressed by jurists that emphasize that the guardianship of the jurist is not a novel concept in Shīʻī thought; it is rather embedded therein, despite the diverse ways of articulating the scope of this guardianship. This pushes the study toward the third question, which we have mentioned regarding the scope of the jurist's guardianship according to Āyatullāh Sayyid Khumaynī, which we will present in the chapter below.

---

[22] al-Muẓaffar, Muḥammad Riḍā, ʻAqāʼid al-Imāmiyyah, (L.T), Qum, Intishārāt Anṣāriyyān, (L.T), page 34.

The Scope of the Guardianship of the Jurist

It is clear to whoever contemplates the aforementioned rational evidence presented by Āyatullāh Sayyid Khumaynī that it is specified within the scope of the interest of the Islāmic community. According to the original terminology, rational evidence is substantial instead of verbal evidence. Substantial evidence is limited to the scope of absolute certainty, for it does not possess a tongue that can expand its scope of inclusivity as can the verbal evidence that can be referred to its generality or absoluteness to infer the wideness of the scope. Therefore, the rational evidence for the jurist's guardianship is limited to a certain social scope, which, in itself, is wide. Nonetheless, it does not include all that lies within the privileges of the Prophet ﷺ or immaculate Imām ؑ.

To clarify this issue, we present the example of offensive jihād. Based on the rational evidence, does it fall within the scope of the jurist's guardianship?

The answer will be no after reflecting on the aforementioned (reasoning). Accordingly, Āyatullāh Sayyid Khumaynī's opinion is that the jurist does not have guardianship over the offensive jihād. This is clear based on the rational evidence for the jurist's guardianship, which is limited to absolute certainty, considering that it is substantial and does not have a tongue whose absoluteness can be referred to by including offensive jihād. Yes, one can mention its inclusivity under the jurist's guardianship in light of narrative evidence, such as the narration by Shaykh Ṣadūq that Āyatullāh Sayyid Khumaynī adopted as narrative evidence for the jurist's guardianship. It is as follows: "Imām 'Alī ﷺ said: the Messenger of God ﷺ said: O' God, have mercy on my successors. Someone said: O' Messenger of God, who are your successors? He said: Those who come after me and narrate – on my behalf – my words and Sunnah."[23] One can refer to the absoluteness that is present therein to prove that the jurists' successorship of the Messenger of God ﷺ includes offensive jihād, based on the premise that this sort of jihād is permissible in Islām and included within the privilege of the immaculate person – which is well-known.[24]

---

[23] Ṣadūq, Shaykh Muḥammad b. 'Alī, *Man Lā Yaḥḍuruh al-Faqīh*, 2nd edition, Qum, published by a group of teachers, 1404 AH, Vol. 4, p. 420.

[24] Review: Barakāt, Shaykh Akram, *al-Takfīr: Ḍawābiṭ al-Islām wa Tatbīqāt al-Muslimīn*, 4th edition, Bayrūt, Bayt al-Sirāj lil Thaqāfah wal-Nashr, p. 200-206.

In addition to the above, it is also clear that the scope of the guardianship of the jurist excludes two other matters that belong to the Prophet ﷺ and the immaculate Imām ؏, which are:

First, the special knowledge-based position is related to the conveyance of the Sharīʿa by the Prophet ﷺ and its actual preservation by the immaculate Imāms ؏. The jurist does not have this role, whether a guardian or otherwise. He rather exerts his utmost efforts in pursuit of realizing the correct Sharīʿa. His conclusions are a matter of deriving its (the Sharīʿa's) rulings based on his understanding. He is not infallible, thereof, in reaching the truth. This is the reason behind the adoption of the concept of 'wronging' in the Shīʿī creed, which believes in the infallibility of the Imāms. This means that the legal rulings are one according to God ﷻ, the noble Messenger ﷺ, and the immaculate Imāms ؏; they neither alter nor change. Moreover, after the jurist exerts the required efforts to realize them, he may succeed in reaching reality or make a mistake without affecting the legitimacy of his legal opinions or rulings.

Second, the special moral position of the Prophet ﷺ and the Imāms ؏ regarding the guardianship of the jurist has no relation to it whatsoever. Therefore, Āyatullāh Sayyid Khumaynī said: "And no one should assume that the entitlement of the jurist for guardianship raises him to the position of prophethood or the position of the Imāms ﷺ. Our discussion here does not tackle the position or level; rather, it tackles the practical role."[25] He also said: "And the confirmation of the guardianship and government to the Imām ﷺ does not mean that he is disconnected from his position with God, and it does not put him at the same level with other rulers. The Imām has a praise-worthy position, a noble status, and a formative vicegerency, which possesses guardianship and control to which all the atoms of the universe submit. Moreover, one of the essentials of our creed is that our Imāms have a position that cannot be reached by any close angel or sent Prophet. Based on the narrations and ḥadīths that we have, the great Messenger ﷺ and Imāms ﷺ were lights - before this world – then God placed them around his throne and conferred upon them a position and level of proximity which

---

[25] Khumaynī, Āyatullāh Sayyid Rūḥullāh Mūsawī, *Ḥukūmat Islāmiyyah*, p. 53.

no one but God knew of.[26] Moreover, as mentioned in the narrations of the Ascent (al-Miʿrāj), Jibrāʾīl (Gabriel) said: (Had I come to a fingertip closer, I would have burnt.)[27] It was also mentioned that they ﷺ said: (We have conditions with God which a close angel or a sent prophet cannot meet.)[28] The same position exists for

---

[26] Ṣaffār, Muḥammad b. Ḥassan, *Baṣāʾir al-Darajāt*, (L.T.), Tehrān, Dār al-ʿAlamī, 1404 AH, Vol. 1, p. 20, section 10.

Majlisī, ʿAllāmah Muḥammad Bāqir, *Biḥār al-Anwār*, Vol. 25, p. 130.

[27] Majlisī, ʿAllamah Muḥammad Bāqir, *Biḥār al-Anwār*, Vol. 18, p. 382.

[28] Check out: Majlisī, ʿAllāmah Muḥammad Bāqir, *Kitāb al-Arbaʿīn*, (L.T.), Qum, al-Maṭbaʿa al-ʿIlmiyyah, 1399 AH, the explanation of the ḥadīth 15, p. 177, with minimal change in the expression. It is mentioned therein that the Prophet ﷺ said: "I share times with God which cannot be met by a close angel or a sent prophet."

Ṣaffār, Muḥammad b. Ḥassan, *Baṣāʾir al-Darajāt*, p. 23, section 11.

Sayyidah Fāṭimah al-Zahrā' [29], not in the sense that she is a vicegerent, ruler, or judge; for this position is another thing beyond guardianship, vicegerency, and government."[30]

Based on the above, one can define the scope of the guardianship of the jurist with its specialization in matters of the political government of the nation, which is one of the privileges of the Prophet and the Imāms. The rational evidence presented by Āyatullāh Sayyid Khumaynī for the guardianship of the jurist is the same rational evidence for the political guardianship of the Prophet and Imāms. For, the knowledge of the Prophet and the Imāms is real, and that of the jurist is apparent. Moreover, the root cause behind the trustworthiness of the Prophet and Imāms in

---

[29] Ṣadūq, Shaykh Muḥammad b. ʿAlī, *ʿIlal al-Sharāiʿ*, (L.T.), Ashraf, published by the Ḥaydariyyah Library, 1966 A.D., Vol. 1, p. 123, ḥadith 1.

Ṣadūq, Shaykh Muḥammad b. ʿAlī, *Maʿānī al-Akhbār*, verified by ʿAlī Akbar al-Ghafāri, (L.T.), Qum, Institute of Islāmic Publishing, 1379 AH, p. 64 and 107.

Majlisī, ʿAllamah Muḥammad Bāqir, *Biḥār al-Anwār*, Vol. 43, p. 12.

[30] Khumaynī, Āyatullāh Sayyid Rūḥullāh Mūsawī, *Ḥukūmat Islāmiyyah,*, p. 56.

applying the (Islāmic) rulings is infallibility, whereas with the jurist, it is justice. As for the evidence, it is the same. This is what Āyatullāh Sayyid Khumaynī meant when he said: "...That which is proof for the Imāmate is, in itself, proof for the necessity of the government after the occultation of the Guardian ﷻ."[31]

The above drives the discussion towards the fourth question we presented in the introduction: If the proposition of the jurist's guardianship is evident for those who are knowledgeable in the rulings and theologies of Islām and embedded within Shīʿī thought, as mentioned prominently by the jurists of the Imāmate school, what then is the reason for its alienation?

This is what we will discuss in the next chapter.

---

[31] Khumaynī, Āyatullāh Sayyid Rūḥullāh Mūsawī, *Kitāb al-Bayʿ*, Vol. 2, p. 461.

Reasons for the Alienation of the Jurist's Guardianship

In his statement above, Āyatullāh Sayyid Khumaynī pointed out the reason behind the alienation of the jurist's guardianship: "... However, the condition of the Islāmic community and that of our academic institutions, in particular, have distanced this topic from the minds to the extent that, today, it needs proof."[32]

Āyatullāh Sayyid Khumaynī elaborated on these two reasons, as we will observe in the detailed presentation below on the reasons behind the alienation of the guardianship of the jurist, which we will present under two titles:

The Internal Factors

A set of factors within the Islāmic community contributed to alienating the jurist's guardianship. Even though some of these factors did not aim intentionally towards distancing the nation from the Islāmic government – in addition to the jurist's guardianship – they influenced the occurrence of that alienation. Some of these factors are:

32 Khumaynī, Āyatullāh Sayyid Rūḥullāh Mūsawī, *Ḥukūmat Islāmiyyah,*, p. 9.

1. Misapplication in Systems that Claim its
    Compliance to Islām

People have witnessed a negative experience in countries that claimed to govern in the name of Islām. Moreover, this misapplication was accompanied by media distortion, which aimed at inflating this experience so that people would rebel against the idea of an Islāmic government.

2. The Religious Publications during the Recent
    Times

Āyatullāh Sayyid Khumaynī pointed out the huge difference between the Noble Qurʾān, modern books, jurisprudential practical letters, and other religious publications.

For, the Qurʾān and books of narrations are richer in writings related to sociology, economics, management and community politics, and human rights than in writings related to the individualistic aspect of a person. Meanwhile, the practical academic letters – presented and mentioned in advanced seminary writings related to Baḥth al-Khārij – focus more on the individualistic than the social aspects. It is also clear that it has an impact on the Perception of the government of Islām in the community.

3. The Guardianship of the Jurist in the Book of Gains (*al-Makāsib*)

Perhaps one of the things that contributed to the alienation of the jurist's guardianship is what has been understood from one of the seminary books that seminary students are still studying since its widespread presence in the seminary during the time of its Chief, Shaykh Murtaḍā al-Anṣārī, who was born in 1214 AH and died in 1281 AH. This book is called *al-Makāsib*.

Although Shaykh al-Anṣārī was one of the adopters of the general guardianship of the jurist – as declared in some of his books[33] - nonetheless, in his book *al-Makāsib* and in the way through which he aimed at sharpening the minds of students of knowledge, he discussed the narrative proofs for the guardianship of the jurist in terms of reference and indication, based on two meanings:

---

[33] Review: al-Anṣārī, Shaykh Murtaḍā, *al-Qaḍā' wal-Shahādāt*, verified by the investigative committee of the works of Shaykh al-Aʿẓam, 1st edition, 1415 AH, p. 48-49.

First: The autonomy of the guardian in disposition, in the sense that he originally has an independent right since he is the right owner thereof. This is the meaning of absolute guardianship, which matches the guardianship of the Imāms ﷺ.

Second: To have the right of disposition, not in the autonomous meaning mentioned above, but rather in the sense that someone else's action is not permissible except with his permission.[34]

He also discussed the indication of the narrative proofs to the first meaning while basing it on the original principle that no one has guardianship over another. Therefore, no proof was concluded by him on the matter. He also harshly emphasized the lack of proof by saying: "And all in all, providing proof for the obligatory submission to the jurist as to the Imām ﷺ – save that which was

---

[34] Review: al-Anṣārī, Shaykh Murtaḍā, *al-Makāsib*, verified by the Investigative Committee of the Works of Shaykh al-Aʿẓam, 2nd edition, Qum, the International Conference in Celebration of the 100th Memorial Day of the Birth of Shaykh al-Anṣārī, Vol. 3, p. 546.

based on evidence – is as difficult as peeling a thorny tree."[35]

The simile above implies peeling a tree with thorns by the palm.[36]

As for the second meaning, Shaykh al-Anṣārī discussed the proofs mentioned thereof, according to his Perception, and reached the following conclusion:

"To any extent, based on those above, it has been shown that these proofs verified the guardianship of the jurist in matters where the legitimacy of creating them, in reality, is a foregone conclusion, such that had there been no jurist people would have been obligated to carry them out as a matter of sufficient duty."[37]

In conclusion, in his book *al-Makāsib*, Shaykh al-Anṣārī did not reject the guardianship of the jurist at all; he rather accepted it in all the matters which

---

[35] Ibid., p. 553.

[36] al-Farāhīdī, al-Khalīl b. Aḥmad, *al-ʿAyn*, Vol. 4, p. 215.

al-Jawharī, Ismāʿīl b. Ḥammād, *al-Siḥāḥ*, Vol. 2, p. 512.

[37] al-Anṣārī, Shaykh Murtaḍā, *Farāʾid al-ʿUṣūl* Vol. 3, p. 555.

have the permissibility of being established outside - nay obligation even in the absence of a jurist – however, he did not accept the idea that the guardian's autonomous right of disposition is similar to the autonomous guardianship of the Prophet ﷺ and the Imāms ؏.

The Impact of *al-Makāsib* on the Perception Toward the Guardianship of the Jurist

This study of the jurist's guardianship greatly impacted the seminary students' Perception of the general guardianship of the jurist in terms of religious proof. This is the conclusion we have reached based on the following points:

a. The book *al-Makāsib* is still being taught in the seminaries until now for the last 150 years.

b. The seminary student studies this book before his knowledge-based mindset unfolds and pulls him out of the circle of astonishment and emulation.

c. Shaykh al-Anṣārī has a strong academic influence in the seminary. In regard to the principles of Islāmic jurisprudence, he is well-known to the extent that the plain title

'Shaykh' refers to him. Moreover, he owns the title 'al-Shaykh al-Aʿẓam,' or the Greatest Shaykh.

d. Besides his academic influence, he is well known for his noble ethics, which made him a unique role model for students of religious studies. This adds to the influence of his speech on seminary students.

Accordingly, the book *al-Makāsib* impacted the seminary students' Perception of the jurist's guardianship.

4. The Repercussions of the Revolution of 1920

Many seminary students experienced a state of social isolation and rejection of novelty for tens of years after the revolution of 1920, which was considered one of the pride of the academic seminary in Najaf. Some of the things reported by those who lived during that period were the objection against whoever kept up with political news in newspapers or otherwise, the rejection of enrolling children in academic schools, the feeling of extreme surprise to see someone wearing a wristwatch or replacing 'al-madras.'[38] With modern shoes... etc.

Some people attributed this situation to the reaction of some of the seminary students after the revolution of 1920 ended in military failure, despite being a pride for al-ʿIrāqiyyūn and their honorable seminary.

For in 1914, the British occupied al-Fāw.[39] And then Baṣrah. Despite the massive suffering endured by al-ʿIrāqiyyūn (ʿIrāqis) due to al-Atrāk (Turks), the academic seminary decided to stand by them to confront the invasion by the British. Thus, the great religious references in Najaf, Karbalāʾ, and Kāẓimiyah declared their legal opinions (fatwa), which mandated the country's defense and fighting the disbelievers and invaders. On top of them was Āyatullāh Mīrza Muḥammad Taqī Shirāzī (Sāmarrāʾ), Āyatullāh Sayyid Muḥammad Kāẓim Ṭabāṭabāʾī Yazdī (Najaf) and Sayyid Mahdī al-Ḥaydarī (Kāẓimiyya). Furthermore, religious scholars did not stop at declaring their legal opinions; they also participated directly in the

---

[38] A type of old shoes.

[39] Kāẓim, ʿAbbās, the revolution of the 15th of Shaʿbān, 1st edition, (L.M.), (L.N.), 1984 A.D., p. 66.

battle. Sayyid Muṣṭafa Kāshānī moved from Najaf to Kāẓimiyya, in addition to Āyatullāh Sayyid ʿAlī al-Dāmād Shaykh Muḥammad Ḥusayn al-Nāʾīnī. Moreover, Āyatullāh Sayyid Muḥammad Yazdī and Āyatullāh Mīrza Shirāzī sent their children to participate in the jihād. Sayyid Mahdī al-Ḥaydarī and Shaykh Mahdī al-Khāliṣī moved from Kāẓimiyah, and Shaykh Muḥammad Saʿīd al-Ḥabūbī moved from Najaf passing through the cities of the middle of al-Furāt to stimulate the audiences, collect weapons and armory and organize the men in divisions for jihād.[40]

After the fall of the Turkish state and establishment of the British occupation, Āyatullāh Mīrza Shirāzī declared his ruling to go to jihād by saying: "If the British insist on taking away your right and keep meeting your pleadings with war, then you must defend (your rights) with all your might; and it is forbidden to submit or yield to them."[41]

Accordingly, the revolution of 1920 rose against the British occupation, led by the scholars of the academic seminary. However, the power imbalance

---

[40] Kāẓim, ʿAbbās, the revolution of the 15th of Shaʿbān, p. 68.

[41] Ibid., p. 290.

between both parties, the absence of the leader – due to the demise of Āyatullāh Mīrzā Muḥammad Taqī Shirāzī and later on Shaykh Muḥammad Ḥusayn al-Nāʾīnī, which could be a secretive assassination – and other reasons, the British managed to destroy the revolution and terrorize the areas of the revolution where the main centers of the academic seminaries were established. Afterward, many of the seminary students underwent social isolation and focused on the knowledge-based aspect away from the general issues of the community.

The perception towards the movement of Āyatullāh Shahīd Sayyid Muḥammad Bāqir al-Ṣadr, which stemmed from the rejection of that reality, is a great indicator of the social effects that unfolded in the seminary during the period that followed the revolution of 1920. This issue kept it extremely far away from raising matters related to the Islāmic government and raised the alienation of studying the guardianship of the jurist.

External Factors

In addition to the above, Āyatullāh Sayyid Khumaynī presented a set of external factors which led to the alienation of the jurist's guardianship.

These factors included the role of the Zionist Jews and the colonization in distancing the Muslim community from the thought of establishing an Islāmic government. From the beginning of its rise, the Islāmic movements were inflicted with the Jews who started their counter-activities against these movements in pursuit of faulting and distorting the reputation of Islām, which still goes on until this very day.

In addition to them, the colonizers realized that the biggest barrier for them in reaching their goals was Islām – including its provisions and theologies. Therefore, they conspired and plotted schemes against it.

The colonizers resorted to the support of the media platforms, educational curricula, and other means to accomplish their goals while focusing on the well-educated Muslims so that they could deviate them – as much as possible – away from the true Islām of the Prophet Muḥammad ﷺ.

Moreover, they implanted fallacies amongst Muslims in pursuit of distorting the image of Islām in their minds, such as:

1. Separating Islām from the system of government and limiting it to individual rulings. Moreover, when they get confronted with (Islāmic) social legislation, they say its execution is unfeasible; thus, the role of Islām gets restricted - at most – to legislation.

2. The harshness of Islāmic judicial rulings led to stipulating new constitutions and laws imported from the West.

3. The unfairness of Islāmic rulings, such as those related to women and the inheritance system.

After this presentation and analysis, the last question mentioned in the introduction remains: What message did Āyatullāh Sayyid Khumaynī want to send by emphasizing the self-evidence of the jurist's guardianship for a person knowledgeable in Islām? This will be tackled in the next chapter.

Impact of the Self-Evidence of the Jurist's Guardianship

The rational evidence adopted by Āyatullāh Sayyid Khumaynī to prove the jurist's guardianship was characterized by several features, two of which will be highlighted below.

First, Generally, absolute rational evidence takes precedence over verbal evidence. If a rational proof is established for a certain proposition, the verbal proof is considered merely supportive and guiding towards the former. Therefore, verbal evidence comes in second place. It is a well-known principle that if the verbal proof conflicts with the rational proof, it should be interpreted according to the latter, and if this is not possible, then it will be rejected.

Second, it has been mentioned above that Āyatullāh Sayyid Khumaynī presented the rational proof under the title of its evidence, which has a special and crucial impact on the connection between the nation and the guardian jurist. It is well-known that following the jurist (*taqlīd*) is limited to the unnecessities of religion. In contrast, regarding the necessities of religion, there is no need to refer to the jurist. Therefore, the dutiful person who believes in its evidence acts upon his belief without asking or resorting to the Marjiʿiyyat. Accordingly, Āyatullāh Sayyid Khumaynī's proposition of the jurist's guardianship as an evident concept makes the connection with the guardian jurist within the scope of the connection with the Marjiʿiyyat and not outside it.

What further clarifies the jurist's guardianship to the believer is that the proof for taqlīd stems from the rational observation of the biographies of rational people, where non-specialists refer to specialists. Therefore, the follower – through his taqlīd – acts from his analysis of absolute reason. Accordingly, he is in the same situation as following a jurist based on his belief and interpretation of absolute reason. Just as the relation between the follower and the Marjiʿiyyat is based on rational proof, likewise is the relation between the nation – who believes through reasonable evidence in the jurist's guardianship – and the guardian jurist. This liberates the nation with this firm belief from the subordination to the Marjiʿiyyat in its Perception of the jurist's guardianship. Thus, the jurist's guardianship is no longer at the mercy of the Marjiʿiyyat's ruling (Ijtihād).

On the contrary, each jurist - the Marjiʿ and the guardian - will have his role regarding their relationship with the Shīʿīs. For, the jurist who is a Marjiʿ will be responsible for the legal opinions (Fatwā), and the guardian jurist will take care of the guardianship-related rulings, in which the guardian jurist shall observe - in addition to the legal proofs – the general interests of the nation that are related to time and space. This disconnects the Marjiʿ from the guardian so that the guardianship no longer passes through the channel of the Marjiʿiyyat. Additionally, this eliminates the requirement of unifying the Marjiʿiyyat and guardianship in one person, which was established out of fear of the Marjiʿiyyat's Perception of the nation's subordination to the guardian jurist. Rather, in this case, the jurist's guardianship is general for the entire nation, including the Marjiʿiyyat.

Conclusion

The illustrated proposition of the jurist's guardianship places it back in its original position from which it was alienated for reasons that were partially mentioned. This guardianship, which observes the human community in its large scenery, sets out the priorities and strategic causes that fulfill the progress of man's willful and social perfection in pursuit of realizing the emergence of this religion and its prevalence over all other religions within the awaited state of justice led by its Chief who awaits from the nation to lay down its preliminary foundations.